WHAT'S THE DIFFERENCE?

WHAT'S THE DIFFERENCE?

*Manhood and Womanhood Defined
According to the Bible*

JOHN PIPER

Foreword by Elisabeth Elliot

CROSSWAY BOOKS

A PUBLISHING MINISTRY OF
GOOD NEWS PUBLISHERS
WHEATON, ILLINOIS

What's the Difference?

Copyright © 1990 by the
Council on Biblical Manhood and Womanhood.

Published by Crossway Books
        a publishing ministry of Good News Publishers
        1300 Crescent Street
        Wheaton, Illinois 60187

Adapted from a chapter in *Recovering Biblical Manhood and Womanhood,* edited by Wayne Grudem and John Piper (Crossway Books, 1990)

The Council on Biblical Manhood and Womanhood was established in 1987 for the purpose of studying and setting forth Biblical teachings on the relationship between men and women, especially in the home and the church.

Cover design: Cindy Kiple

First printing, trade paper edition, 2001

Printed in the United States of America

Library of Congress Catalog Card Number 90-80358

ISBN 13: 978-1-58134-291-8

ISBN 10: 1-58134-291-8

VP		17	16	15	14	13	12	11	10	09	08	07
20	19	18	17	16	15	14	13	12	11	10	9	

To Noël
my partner
in the great mystery

Contents

FOREWORD BY *Elisabeth Elliot*   9

1   WHAT'S THE DIFFERENCE?   11

2   THE MEANING OF MASCULINITY   23

3   THE MEANING OF FEMININITY   49

4   THE BIBLICAL VISION OF COMPLEMENTARITY   65

5   A CLOSING CHALLENGE TO MEN AND WOMEN   71

NOTES   83

A NOTE ON RESOURCES   92
    Desiring God Ministries

Foreword

For years I have noted with growing disquiet the pollution of many Christians' minds by the doctrine of feminism. I believe it is a far more dangerous pollution than most have realized, and I (with what seemed to me pitifully few others) have tried to sound the alarm in every way I could. It is a relief to me that John Piper has done what was badly needed—clarified the fundamental distinctions, defining them not fashionably but Biblically and with good common sense. He has done more—he has cut through much of the confusion that arises through a careless reading of the "difficult" Bible passages, and shown us the true liberation that comes with humble submission to God's original design. I think his thesis rings true to the manliness or the womanliness in each of us.

—*Elisabeth Elliot*

1

What's the Difference?

When I was a boy growing up in Greenville, South Carolina, my father was away from home about two-thirds of every year. And while he preached across the country, we prayed—my mother and my older sister and I. What I learned in those days was that my mother was omni-competent.

She handled the finances, paying all the bills and dealing with the bank and creditors. She once ran a little laundry business on the side. She was active on the park board, served as the superintendent of the intermediate department of our Southern Baptist church, and managed some real estate holdings.

She taught me how to cut the grass and splice electric cord and pull Bermuda grass by the roots and paint the eaves and shine the dining-room table with a shammy and drive a car and keep French fries from getting soggy in the cooking oil. She helped me with the maps in geography and showed me how to do a bibliography and work up a science project on static electricity and believe that Algebra II was possible. She dealt with the contractors when we added a basement and, more than once, put her hand to the shovel. It never occurred to me that there was anything she couldn't do.

I heard one time that women don't sweat, they glow. Not true. My mother sweated. It would drip off the end of her long, sharp nose. Sometimes she would blow it off when her hands were pushing the wheelbarrow full of peat moss. Or she would wipe it with her sleeve between the strokes of a swingblade. Mother was strong. I can remember her arms even today thirty years later. They were big, and in the summertime they were bronze.

But it never occurred to me to think of my mother and my father in the same category. Both were strong. Both were bright. Both were kind. Both would kiss me and both would spank me. Both were good with words. Both prayed with fervor and loved the Bible. But unmistakably my father was a man and my mother was a woman. They knew it and I knew it. And it was not mainly a biological fact. It was mainly a matter of personhood and relational dynamics.

When my father came home he was clearly the head of the house. He led in prayer at the table. He called the family together for devotions. He got us to Sunday School and worship. He drove the car. He guided the family to where we would sit. He made the decision to go to Howard Johnson's for lunch. He led us to the table. He called for the waitress. He paid the check. He was the one we knew we would reckon with if we broke a family rule or were disrespectful to Mother. These were the happiest times for Mother. Oh, how she rejoiced to have Daddy home! She loved his leadership. Later I learned that the Bible calls this "submission."

But since my father was gone most of the time, Mother used to do most of those leadership things too. So it never occurred to me that leadership and submission had anything to do with superiority and inferiority. And it didn't have to do with muscles and skills either. It was not a matter of capabilities and competencies. It had to do with something I could never have explained as a child. And I have been a long time in coming to understand it as part of God's great goodness in creating us male and female. It had to do with something very deep. I know that the specific rhythm of life that was in our home is not the only good one. But there were dimensions of reality and goodness in it that ought to be there in every home. Indeed they ought to be there in varying ways in all mature relationships between men and women.

I say "ought to be there" because I now see that they were rooted in God. Over the years I have come to see from Scripture and from life that manhood and womanhood are the beautiful handiwork of a good and loving God. He designed our differences and they are profound. They are not mere physiological prerequisites for sexual union. They go to the root of our personhood. This essay is an attempt to define some of those differences as God wills them to be according to the Bible.

* * * * *

Let me say a word about that phrase, "according to the Bible." The subtitle of this little book is "Manhood and Womanhood Defined *According to the Bible*." What that means is that I have made every effort to bring the thinking of this book into accord with what the Bible teaches. At the same time, however, I have not tried to include a detailed exegetical argument for every assertion.

There are two main reasons that seem to justify this approach:

First, for the purposes of this little book, it seemed best to present the Biblical vision of manhood and womanhood as clearly and concisely as possible, and to leave the comprehensive technical discussion for other publications. Thus this little book was originally written as a chapter in a larger collection of essays, *Recovering Biblical Manhood and Womanhood* (published in 1990 by Crossway Books; edited by Wayne Grudem and John Piper), and this longer work provides detailed exegetical support for the vision of this smaller work.

I have also tried in articles,[1] sermons,[2] and unpublished papers to give a credible account of the Biblical foundations of what I say here.

Second, I have tried to include enough Biblical argumentation in this essay, especially in the footnotes, to show why I believe this vision of manhood and womanhood is in fact *"according to the Bible."* I hope it will be obvious that my reflections are not the creation of an independent mind, but the fruit of a tree planted firmly in the soil of constant meditation on the Word of God.

Third, experience has taught me that there are two ways to commend a vision of manhood and womanhood. One way has to do with rational argumentation concerning factual evidences. For example, an evangelical Christian wants to know, Does the Bible really teach this vision of manhood and womanhood? So one way of commending the vision is by patient, detailed, careful exegetical argumentation.

But there is another way to commend the vision. A person also wants to know, Is the vision beautiful and satisfying and fulfilling? Can I live with it? This is not a bad question. Commending Biblical truth involves more than saying, "Do it because the Bible says so." That sort of commendation may result in a kind of obedience that is so begrudging and so empty of delight and hearty affirmation that the Lord is not pleased with it at all.

So there is a second task needed in winning people over

to a vision of manhood and womanhood. Not only must there
be thorough exegesis, there must also be a portrayal of the
vision that satisfies the heart as well as the head. Or to put it
another way: we must commend the beauty as well as the
truth of the vision. We must show that something is not only
right but also good. It is not only valid but also valuable, not
only accurate but also admirable.

This little book is meant to fit *mainly* into the second category. Not merely, but mainly. It is designed to show that our
vision of manhood and womanhood is a deeply satisfying gift
of grace from a loving God who has the best interests of his
creatures at heart. The vision is not onerous or oppressive. It
does not promote pride or self-exaltation. It conforms to who
we are by God's good design. Therefore it is fulfilling in the
deepest sense of that word.

* * * * *

The tendency today is to stress the equality of men and
women by minimizing the unique significance of our maleness or femaleness. But this depreciation of male and female
personhood is a great loss. It is taking a tremendous toll on
generations of young men and women who do not know what
it means to be a man or a woman. Confusion over the meaning of sexual personhood today is epidemic. The consequence
of this confusion is not a free and happy harmony among gen-

der-free persons relating on the basis of abstract competencies. The consequence rather is more divorce, more homosexuality, more sexual abuse, more promiscuity, more social awkwardness, and more emotional distress and suicide that come with the loss of God-given identity.

It is a remarkable and telling observation that contemporary Christian feminists devote little attention to the definition of femininity and masculinity. Little help is being given to a son's question, "Dad, what does it mean to be a man and not a woman?" Or a daughter's question, "Mom, what does it mean to be woman and not a man?" A lot of energy is being expended today minimizing the distinctions of manhood and womanhood. But we do not hear very often what manhood and womanhood *should* incline us to do. We are adrift in a sea of confusion over sexual roles. And life is not the better for it.

Ironically the most perceptive thinkers recognize how essential manhood and womanhood are to our personhood. Yet the meaning of manhood and womanhood is seen as unattainable. For example, Paul Jewett, in his very insightful book, *Man as Male and Female*, argues persuasively that maleness and femaleness are essential, not peripheral, to our personhood:

> Sexuality permeates one's individual being to its very depth; it conditions every facet of one's life as a person. As the self is always aware of itself as an 'I,' so this 'I' is always aware of itself as *himself* or *herself*. Our self-

knowledge is indissolubly bound up not simply with our *human* being but with our *sexual* being. At the human level there is no 'I and thou' *per se*, but only the 'I' who is male or female confronting the 'thou,' the 'other,' who is also male or female.[3]

He cites Emil Brunner to the same effect: "Our sexuality penetrates to the deepest metaphysical ground of our personality. As a result, the physical differences between the man and the woman are a parable of psychical and spiritual differences of a more ultimate nature."[4]

After reading these amazing statements concerning how essential manhood and womanhood are to our personhood and how sexuality "conditions every facet of one's life," it is stunning to read that Jewett does not know what manhood and womanhood are. He says,

> Some, at least, among contemporary theologians are not so sure that they know what it means to be a man in distinction to a woman or a woman in distinction to a man. It is because the writer shares this uncertainty that he has skirted the question of ontology in this study.[5]
>
> All human activity reflects a qualitative distinction which is sexual in nature. But in my opinion, such an observation offers no clue to the ultimate meaning of that distinction. It may be that we shall never know what that distinction ultimately means. But this much, at least, seems clear: we will understand the difference— what it means to be created as man or woman— only as we learn to live as man and woman in a true partnership of life.[6]

Surely this is a great sadness. We know that "sexuality permeates one's individual being to its very depth." We know that "it conditions every facet of one's life as a person." We know that every I-Thou encounter is an encounter not of abstract persons but of male or female persons. We know that physical differences are but a parable of male and female personhood. But, alas, we do not know who we are as male and female. We are ignorant of this all-pervasive dimension of our identity.

But what about Jewett's prescription for hope in the face of this stunning ignorance of who we are? He suggests that we discover who we are "as man or woman" by experiencing a "true partnership" as man *and* woman. The problem with this is that we cannot know what a "true partnership" is until we know the nature of the partners. A true partnership must be true to who the partners are. A true partnership must take into account the sexual reality "that conditions every facet of their life." We simply cannot know what a "true" partnership is until we know what truly "permeates [our] personhood to the very depths." If we are really ignorant of what true manhood and womanhood are, we have no warrant to prescribe the nature of what *true* partnership will look like.

The sexual turmoil of our culture is not surprising when we discover that our best Christian thinkers claim not to know what masculinity and femininity are, and yet acknowledge that these are among the most profound aspects of personhood that "condition every facet of one's life"! How shall parents rear daughters to be women and sons to be men when even the leading teachers of the church do not know what manhood and womanhood are?

The conviction behind this essay is that the Bible does not leave us in ignorance about the meaning of masculine and feminine personhood. God has not placed in us an all-pervasive and all-conditioning dimension of personhood and then hidden the meaning of our identity from us. He has shown us in Scripture the beauty of manhood and womanhood in complementary harmony. He has shown us the distortions and even horrors that sin has made of fallen manhood and womanhood. And he has shown us the way of redemption and healing through Christ.

To be sure, we see "through a glass dimly." Our knowledge is not perfect. We must be ever open to new light. But we are not so adrift as to have nothing to say to our generation about the meaning of manhood and womanhood and its implications for our relationships. Our understanding is that the Bible reveals the nature of masculinity and femininity by describing diverse responsibilities for man and woman while rooting these differing responsibilities in creation, not convention.

When the Bible teaches that men and women fulfil different roles in relation to each other, charging man with a unique leadership role, it bases this differentiation not on temporary cultural norms but on permanent facts of creation. This is seen in 1 Corinthians 11:3-16 (especially vv. 8-9, 14); Ephesians 5:21-33 (especially vv. 31-32); and 1 Timothy 2:11-14 (especially vv. 13-14).[7] In the Bible, differentiated roles for men and women are never traced back to the fall of man and woman into sin. Rather, the foundation of this differentiation is traced back to the way things were in Eden before sin warped our relationships. Differentiated roles were corrupted, not created, by the fall.[8] They were created by God.

* * * * *

This leads me then to attempt at least a partial definition of manhood and womanhood. This is risky business. Every word we choose could be misunderstood. Unsympathetic readers could jump to conclusions about practical implications that are not implied. I would simply plead for the application of that great principle of good criticism: Before assessing an author's position, express an understanding of it in a way the author would approve.

I would commend the following descriptions of masculinity and femininity for consideration. It will be very important to read them in the light of the subsequent comments. These are not exhaustive descriptions of all that masculinity or femininity mean. They are an attempt to get at the heart, or at least an indispensable aspect, of manhood and womanhood.[9]

AT THE HEART OF MATURE MASCULINITY IS A
SENSE OF BENEVOLENT RESPONSIBILITY TO
LEAD, PROVIDE FOR AND PROTECT WOMEN IN
WAYS APPROPRIATE TO A MAN'S DIFFERING RELA-
TIONSHIPS.

AT THE HEART OF MATURE FEMININITY IS A FREE-
ING DISPOSITION TO AFFIRM, RECEIVE AND NUR-
TURE STRENGTH AND LEADERSHIP FROM
WORTHY MEN IN WAYS APPROPRIATE TO A
WOMAN'S DIFFERING RELATIONSHIPS.

2

The Meaning of
Masculinity

Here we take the definition of masculinity a phrase at a time
and unfold its meaning and implications.

> AT THE HEART OF MATURE MASCULINITY IS A
> SENSE OF BENEVOLENT RESPONSIBILITY TO
> LEAD, PROVIDE FOR AND PROTECT WOMEN
> IN WAYS APPROPRIATE TO A MAN'S DIFFERING
> RELATIONSHIPS.

"AT THE HEART OF . . ."

This phrase signals that the definitions are not exhaustive.
There is more to masculinity and femininity, but there is not
less. We believe this is at the heart of what true manhood

means, even if there is a mystery to our complementary existence that we will never exhaust.

". . . MATURE MASCULINITY . . ."

A man might say, "I am a man and I do not feel this sense of responsibility that you say makes me masculine." He may feel strong and sexually competent and forceful and rational. But we would say to him that if he does not feel this sense of benevolent responsibility toward women to lead, provide and protect, his masculinity is immature. It is incomplete and perhaps distorted.

"Mature" means that a man's sense of responsibility is in the process of growing out of its sinful distortions and limitations, and finding its true nature as a form of love, not a form of self-assertion.

". . . A SENSE OF . . ."

I use the word "sense" because to be masculine a man must not only be responsible, but sense or feel that he is. If he does not "sense" or "feel" and "affirm" his responsibility, he is not mature in his masculinity.

The word "sense" also implies the fact that a man can be mature in his masculinity when his circumstances do not put him in any relationship where he actually has the possibility to relate to any woman. He may be in combat or out to sea away from women. He may be in prison. He may have a job on an oil rig in the North Atlantic. He may be a monk. Or his style of life may simply make interaction with women very limited.

A man can be properly masculine in those circumstances if he has the sense of benevolent responsibility to lead, provide for and protect women. This sense need not be actualized directly in order to qualify for mature masculinity. For example, his "sense" of responsibility will affect how he talks about women and the way he relates to pornography and the kind of concern he shows for the marriages of the men around him.

The word "sense" also implies that a man may not be physically able to provide for or protect his family and yet be mature in his masculinity. He may be paralyzed. He may have a disabling disease. His wife may be the main breadwinner in such a circumstance. And she may be the one who must get up at night to investigate a frightening noise in the house. This is not easy for the man. But if he still has a sense of his own benevolent responsibility under God he will not lose his masculinity.

His sense of responsibility will find expression in the ways he conquers self-pity, and gives moral and spiritual *leadership* for his family, and takes the initiative to *provide* them with the bread of life, and *protect* them from the greatest enemies of all, Satan and sin.

Someone might ask: So is a woman masculine if she is a

single parent and provides these same things for her children? Are these only for men to do? I would answer: A woman is not unduly masculine in performing these things for her children if she has the sense that this would be properly done by her husband if she had one, and if she performs them with a uniquely feminine demeanor.

However, if a woman undertakes to give this kind of leadership toward her husband she would not be acting in a properly feminine way, but would be taking up the masculine calling in that relationship. If the husband is there but neglects his responsibility and does not provide leadership for the children, then the mature, feminine mother will make every effort to do so, yet in a way that says to the husband, "I do not defy you, I love you and long with all my heart that you were with me in this spiritual and moral commitment, leading me and the family to God."

". . . BENEVOLENT . . ."

This word is intended to show that the responsibility of manhood is for the *good* of woman. Benevolent responsibility is meant to rule out all self-aggrandizing authoritarianism (cf. Luke 22:26). It is meant to rule out all disdaining condescension and any act that makes a mature woman feel patronized rather than honored and prized (cf. 1 Peter 3:7). The word "benevolent" is meant to signal that mature masculinity gives appropriate expression to the Golden Rule in male-female relationships (Matthew 7:12).

". . . RESPONSIBILITY . . ."

The burden of this word is to stress that masculinity is a God-given *trust* for the good of all his creatures, not a *right* for men to exercise for their own self-exaltation or ego-satisfaction. It is less a prerogative than a calling. It is a duty and obligation and charge. Like all God's requirements it is not meant to be onerous or burdensome (1 John 5:3). But it is nevertheless a burden to be borne, and which in Christ can be borne lightly (Matthew 11:30).

The word "responsibility" is chosen to imply that man will be uniquely called to account for his leadership, provision and protection in relation to women. This is illustrated in Genesis 3:9 when God says to Adam first, "Where are you?" Eve had sinned first, but God does not seek her out first. Adam must give the first account to God for the moral life of the family in the garden of Eden. This does not mean the woman has no responsibility, as we will see. It simply means that man bears a unique and primary one.

". . . TO LEAD . . ."

One problem with language is that words tend to carry very different connotations for different people. Hence the word "lead" will sound strong and domineering to some, but moderate and servant-like to others.

Another problem is that one word carries many different nuances and implications for different contexts and situations. For example, the word "lead" could refer to what people do when they direct an orchestra, or persuade a friend to go to the zoo, or inspire a group for a cause, or command a military platoon, or make the first suggestion about where to eat, or take the driver's seat when a group gets in the car, or take the initiative in a group to push the button in an elevator, or choose a door and open it for another to go through, or chair a committee, or sing loud enough to help others, or point a lost motorist to the freeway entrance, or call the plays on a football team, or call people together for prayer.

Therefore, I need to explain in some detail what I have in mind by the mature masculine responsibility to lead. Otherwise false ideas could easily come into people's minds that I do not intend. Following are nine clarifying statements about the meaning of mature masculine leadership.

1. Mature masculinity expresses itself not in the demand to be served, but in the strength to serve and to sacrifice for the good of woman.

Jesus said, "Let the greatest among you become as the youngest and the leader as one who serves" (Luke 22:26). Leadership is not a demanding demeanor. It is moving things

forward to a goal. If the goal is holiness and Heaven, the leading will have the holy aroma of Heaven about it—the
demeanor of Christ.

Thus after saying that "the husband is the head of the wife
as Christ is the head of the church," Paul said, "Husbands, love
your wives as Christ loved the church and *gave himself up for
her,* that he might sanctify her" (Ephesians 5:23, 25). Jesus led
his bride to holiness and Heaven on the Calvary road. He
looked weak, but he was infinitely strong in saying NO to the
way of the world. So it will be again and again for mature men
as they take up the responsibility to lead.

**2. Mature masculinity does not assume the authority of
Christ over woman, but advocates it.**

The leadership implied in the statement, "The husband is
the head of the wife *as Christ is the head of the church*"
(Ephesians 5:23), is not a leadership that gives to the man all
the rights and authority that Christ has. The analogy between
Christ and the husband breaks down if pressed too far, first
because, unlike Christ, all men sin. Christ never has to apol-
ogize to his church. But husbands must do this often.

Moreover, unlike Christ, a husband is not preparing a
bride merely for himself but for another, namely Christ. He
does not merely act as Christ, but also for Christ. At this
point he must not be Christ to his wife lest he be a traitor to
Christ. Standing in the place of Christ must include a renun-

ciation of the temptation to be Christ. And that means leading his wife forward to depend not on him but on Christ.
And practically, that rules out belittling supervision and fas-
tidious oversight. She also stands or falls before her own
master, Jesus Christ.

3. Mature masculinity does not presume superiority, but mobilizes the strengths of others.

No human leader is infallible. Nor is any man superior to
those he leads in every respect. Therefore a good leader will
always take into account the ideas of those he leads, and may
often adopt those ideas as better than his own. This applies to
husbands at home and elders in the church and all the other
places where leadership is critical.[10] A man's leadership is not
measured by his obliviousness to the ideas and desires of others. A leader of peers may be surrounded by much brighter
people than himself. He will listen and respond. And if he is
a good leader, they will appreciate his initiative and guidance
through the ups and downs of decision-making. The aim of
leadership is not to demonstrate the superiority of the leader,
but to bring out all the strengths of people that will move them
forward to the desired goal.

In Ephesians 5:28-29 the wife is pictured as part of the
man's body as the church is part of Christ's body. So in loving
his wife a man is loving himself. This is clearly an application
to marriage of Jesus' command, "Love your neighbor as your-

self." This rules out a leadership that treats a wife like a child. A husband does not want to be treated that way himself.

Moreover Christ does not lead the church as his daughter but as his wife. He is preparing her to be a "fellow-heir" (Romans 8:17), not a servant girl. Any kind of leadership that in the name of Christlike headship tends to produce in a wife personal immaturity or spiritual weakness or insecurity through excessive control or picky supervision or oppressive domination has missed the point of the analogy in Ephesians 5. Christ does not create that kind of wife.

4. Mature masculinity does not have to initiate every action, but feels the responsibility to provide a general pattern of initiative.

In a family the husband does not do all the thinking and planning. His leadership is to take responsibility *in general* to initiate and carry through the spiritual and moral planning for family life. I say "in general" because "in specifics" there will be many times and many areas of daily life where the wife will do all kinds of planning and initiating. But there is a general tone and pattern of initiative that should develop which is sustained by the husband.

For example, the leadership pattern would be less than Biblical if the wife in general was having to take the initiative in prayer at meal time, and get the family out of bed for worship on Sunday morning, and gather the family for devotions, and discuss what moral standards will be required of the children, and confer about financial priorities, and talk over some neighborhood ministry possibilities, etc. A wife may initiate the discussion and planning of any one of these, but if she becomes the one who senses the general responsibility for this pattern of initiative while her husband is passive, something contrary to Biblical masculinity and femininity is in the offing.[11]

Psychologist James Dobson is so concerned about the recovery of the leadership of husbands at home that he calls it "America's greatest need."

> A Christian man is obligated to lead his family to the best of his ability. . . . If his family has purchased too many items on credit, then the financial crunch is ultimately his fault. If the family never reads the Bible or seldom goes to church on Sunday, God holds the man to blame. If the children are disrespectful and disobedient, the primary responsibility lies with the father . . . not his wife. . . . In my view, America's greatest need is for husbands to begin guiding their families, rather than pouring every physical and emotional resource into the mere acquisition of money.[12]

5. Mature masculinity accepts the burden of the final say in disagreements between husband and wife, but does not presume to use it in every instance.

In a good marriage decision-making is focussed on the husband, but is not unilateral. He seeks input from his wife and often adopts her ideas. This is implied in the love that governs the relationship (Ephesians 5:25), in the equality of personhood implied in being created in the image of God (Genesis 1:27), and in the status of being fellow-heirs of the grace of life (1 Peter 3:7). Unilateral decision-making is not usually a mark of good leadership. It generally comes from laziness or insecurity or inconsiderate disregard.

On the other hand dependence on team input should not go to the point where the family perceives a weakness of indecision in the husband. And both husband and wife should agree on the principle that the husband's decision should rightly hold sway if it does not involve sin. However, this conviction does not mean that a husband will often use the prerogative of "veto" over the wishes of his wife or family. He may, in fact, very often surrender his own preference for his wife's where no moral issue is at stake. His awareness of his sin and imperfection will guard him from thinking that following Christ gives him the ability of Christ to know what's best in every detail. Nevertheless, in a well-ordered Biblical marriage both husband and wife acknowledge in principle that, if necessary in some disagreement, the husband will accept the burden of making the final choice.

6. **Mature masculinity expresses its leadership in romantic sexual relations by communicating an aura of strong and tender pursuit.**

This is very difficult to put into words. But sexual relations are so basic to human life we would be delinquent not to at least try to say how masculinity expresses itself here.

It is the mingling of tenderness with strength that makes the unique masculine quality of leadership in sexual relations. There is an aura of masculine leadership which rises from the mingling of power and tenderness, forcefulness and affection, potency and sensitivity, virility and delicateness. It finds expression in the firmness of his grasp, the strength of taking her in his arms, the sustaining of verbal adoration, etc. And there are a hundred nuances of masculine pursuit that distinguish it from feminine pursuit.

It is important to say that there is, of course, a feminine pursuit in sexual relations. This is why the word "initiate" is not an exact way of describing masculine leadership in sexual relations. The wife may initiate an interest in romance and may keep on initiating different steps along the way. But there is a difference. A feminine initiation is in effect an invitation for the man to do his kind of initiating. In one sense then you could say that in those times the man is *responding*. But in fact the wife is inviting him to lead in a way as only a man can, so that she can respond to him.

It will not do to say that, since the woman can rightly initiate, therefore there is no special leadership that the man should fulfil. When a wife wants sexual relations with her husband she wants him to seek her and take her and bring her into his arms and up to the pleasures that his initiatives give her.

Consider what is lost when women attempt to assume a more masculine role by appearing physically muscular and aggressive. It is true that there is something sexually stimulating about a muscular, scantily clad young woman pumping iron in a health club. But no woman should be encouraged by this fact. For it probably means the sexual encounter that such an image would lead to is something very hasty and volatile, and in the long run unsatisfying. The image of a masculine musculature begets arousal in a man, but it does not beget several hours of moonlight walking with significant, caring conversation. The more women can arouse men by doing typically masculine things, the less they can count on receiving from men a sensitivity to typically feminine needs. Mature masculinity will not be reduced to raw desire in sexual relations. It remains alert to the deeper personal needs of woman and mingles strength and tenderness to make her joy complete.

7. Mature masculinity expresses itself in a family by taking the initiative in disciplining the children when both parents are present and a family standard has been broken.

Mothers and fathers are both to be obeyed by their children (Ephesians 6:1). Mothers as well as fathers are esteemed teachers in the home (Proverbs 1:8; 6:20; 31:1). They carry rights of authority and leadership toward their children, as do their husbands. They do not need to wait till Dad gets home from work to spank a disobedient child.

But children need to see a dynamic between Mom and Dad that says, Dad takes charge to discipline me when Mom and Dad are both present.[13] No woman should have to take the initiative to set a disobedient child right while her husband sits obliviously by, as though nothing were at stake. Few things will help children understand the meaning of responsible, loving masculinity better than watching who takes the responsibility to set them right when Mom and Dad are both present.

8. Mature masculinity is sensitive to cultural expressions of masculinity and adapts to them (where no sin is involved) in order to communicate to a woman that a man would like to relate not in any aggressive or perverted way, but with maturity and dignity as a man.

This would mean dressing in ways that are neither effeminate nor harsh and aggressive. It would mean learning manners and customs. Who speaks for the couple at the restaurant? Who seats the other? Who drives the car? Who opens the door? Who walks in front down the concert hall aisle? Who stands and who sits, and when? Who extends the hand at a greeting? Who walks on the street side? How do you handle a woman's purse? Etc. Etc. These things change from culture to culture and from era to era. The point is that masculine leadership will not scorn them or ignore them, but seek to use them to cultivate and communicate a healthy pattern of complementarity in the relationships between men and women.[14] Mature masculinity will not try to communicate that such things don't matter. Mature masculinity recognizes the pervasive implications of manhood and womanhood, and seeks to preserve the patterns of interaction that give free and natural expression to that reality. A dance is all the more beautiful when the assigned steps are natural and unself-conscious.

9. Mature masculinity recognizes that the call to leadership is a call to repentance and humility and risk-taking.

We are all sinners. Masculinity and femininity have been distorted by our sin. Taking up the responsibility to lead must therefore be a careful and humble task. We must admit as men that historically there have been grave abuses. In each of our lives we have ample cause for contrition at our passivity or our domination. Some have neglected their wives and squandered their time in front of the television or putzing around in the garage or going away too often with the guys to hunt or fish or bowl. Others have been too possessive, harsh, domineering, and belittling, giving the impression through act and innuendo that wives are irresponsible or foolish.

We should humble ourselves before God for our failures and for the remaining tendency to shirk or overstep our responsibilities. The call to leadership is not a call to exalt ourselves over any woman. It is not a call to domineer, or belittle or put woman in her place. She is, after all, a fellow-heir of God and destined for a glory that will one day blind the natural eyes of every man (Matthew 13:43). The call to leadership is a call to humble oneself and take the responsibility to be a servant-leader in ways that are appropriate to every different relationship to women.

It is a call to risk getting egg on our faces; to pray as we have never prayed before; to be constantly in the Word; to be more given to planning, more intentional, more thoughtful, less carried along by the mood of the moment; to be disciplined and ordered in our lives; to be tenderhearted and sensitive; to take the initiative to make sure there is a time and a place to talk to her about what needs to be talked about; and to be ready to lay down our lives the way Christ did if that is necessary.

". . . PROVIDE FOR . . ."

"At the heart of mature masculinity is a sense of benevolent responsibility to lead, *provide for . . .*"

The point of saying that man should feel a responsibility to provide for woman is not that the woman should not assist in maintaining support for the family or for society in general. She always has done this historically because so much of the domestic life required extraordinary labors on her part just to maintain the life of the family. Today in many cultures women carry a tremendous breadwinning role in the field, often while the men do far less strenuous tasks. It is possible to be excessively demanding or excessively restrictive on a woman's role in sustaining the life of the family. Proverbs 31 pictures a wife with great ability in the business affairs of the family.

What I mean when I say that a man should feel a benevolent responsibility to *provide* is this: when there is no bread on the table it is the man who should feel the main pressure to do something to get it there. It does not mean his wife can't help — side by side in a family enterprise or working in a different job. In fact, it is possible to imagine cases where she may have to do it all — say, if he is sick or injured. But a man will feel his personhood compromised if he, through sloth or folly or lack of discipline, becomes dependent over the long haul (not just during graduate school!) on his wife's income.

This is implied in Genesis 3 where the curse touches man and woman in their natural places of life. It is not a curse that man must work in the field to get bread for the family or that woman bears children. The curse is that these spheres of life are made difficult and frustrating. In appointing the curse for his rebellious creatures God aims at the natural sphere of life peculiar to each. Evidently God had in mind from the beginning that the man would take special responsibility for sustaining the family through breadwinning labor, while the wife would take special responsibility for sustaining the family through childbearing and nurturing labor. Both are life-sustaining and essential.

The point of this Genesis text is not to define limits for what else the man and the woman might do. But it does suggest that any role reversal at these basic levels of childcare and breadwinning labor will be contrary to the original intention of God, and contrary to the way he made us as male and female for our ordained roles.[15] Supporting the family is primarily the responsibility of the husband. Caring for the children is primarily the responsibility of the wife.

Again I stress that the point here is not to dictate the details of any particular pattern of labor in the home. The point is that mature manhood senses a benevolent responsibility before God to be the primary provider for his family. He senses that if God were to come and call someone to account for not meeting the family's needs God would come to the husband first (Genesis 3:9).

The same is true for a social grouping of men and women who are not married. Mature men sense that it is primarily (not solely) their responsibility to see to it that there is provision and protection. The covenant of marriage does not create a man's sense of benevolent responsibility to provide the basic necessities of food and shelter. In marriage the sense of responsibility is more intense and personal. But this dimension of mature manhood is there in a man apart from marriage.

". . . PROTECTION . . ."

"At the heart of mature masculinity is a sense of benevolent responsibility to lead, provide for and *protect* . . ."

Suppose a man and a woman (it may be his wife or sister or friend or a total stranger) are walking along the street when an assailant threatens the two of them with a lead pipe. Mature masculinity senses a natural, God-given responsibility to step forward and put himself between the assailant and the woman. In doing this he becomes her servant. He is willing to suffer for her safety. He bestows honor on her. His inner sense is one of responsibility to protect her because he is a man and she is a woman.

There is a distorted and sinful masculinity that might claim an authority and leadership that has the right to tell the woman to step in front of him and shield him from the blows and let him escape. But every man knows this is a perversion of what it means to be a man and a leader. And every wife knows that something is amiss in a man's manhood if he suggests that she get out of bed 50% of the time to see what the strange noise is downstairs.

She is not condemned as a coward because she feels a natural fitness in receiving this manly service. And she may well be more courageous than he at the moment. She may be ready to do some fearless deed of her own. A man's first thought is not that the woman at his side is weak, but simply that he is a man and she is a woman. Women and children are put into the lifeboats first, not because the men are necessarily better swimmers, but because of a deep sense of honorable fitness. It belongs to masculinity to accept danger to protect women.

It may be that in any given instance of danger the woman will have the strength to strike the saving blow. It may be too that she will have the presence of mind to think of the best way of escape. It may be that she will fight with tooth and claw to save a crippled man and lay down her life for him if necessary. But this does not at all diminish the unique call of manhood when he and his female companion are confronted by a danger together. The dynamics of mature masculinity and femininity begin the drama with him in front and her at his back protected—however they may together overcome the foe or suffer courageously together in persecution. A mature man senses instinctively that as a man he is called to take the lead in guarding the woman he is with.[16]

". . . WOMEN . . ."

"At the heart of mature masculinity is a sense of benevolent responsibility to lead, provide for and protect *women . . .*"

I do not say "wives" because there is a sense in which masculinity inclines a man to feel a responsibility for leadership and provision and protection toward women in general, not just toward wives or relatives. Masculinity and femininity are rooted in who we are by nature. They are not simply reflexes of a marriage relationship. Man does not become man by getting married. But it is clear that the *form* which leadership, provision and protection take will vary with the kind of relationship a man has with a woman—from the most intimate relationship of marriage to the most casual relationship with a stranger on the street. This is why the description of masculinity must conclude with the following phrase.

" . . . IN WAYS APPROPRIATE TO A MAN'S DIFFERING RELATIONSHIPS."

Ephesians 5:22, Titus 2:5 and 1 Peter 3:1, 5 exhort wives to be subject to "your own" (*idiois*) husbands. This term, "your own" shows that the relationship of leadership and submission between a woman and her husband should be different from the relationship of leadership and submission which she may have with men in general. Husbands and wives have responsibilities to each other in marriage that they do not have to other men and women.

But this does not mean that there is no way that male-

ness and femaleness affect the relationship of men and
women in general. That a man has a unique responsibility
for leadership in his own home does not mean that his manhood is negligible in other settings. It is not negligible. But
it is very diverse. The responsibility of men toward women
will vary according to the kind of relationship they have.
Husband and wife will have different responsibilities than a
pastor and female parishioner will have. And those responsibilities will in turn be different from the differing responsibilities of men and women in business, recreation,
government, neighborhood, courtship, engagement, etc.
The possibilities of women and men meeting each other and
having dealings with each other are extremely diverse and
beyond counting. And my persuasion is that mature masculinity will seek appropriate expressions of manhood in
each of these relationships.

   These expressions of manhood will include acts of defense
and protection, a readiness to serve with strength, and a pattern of initiative. I have touched on all three of these. But it
may be helpful to focus once more on this idea of a pattern of
initiative that is appropriate for differing relationships. The
point here is that even though a man will not take initiating
steps of leadership with a stranger or with a colleague the same
way he will with his wife, his mature manhood will seek a pattern of initiative appropriate for the relationship.

   For example, if a man works as a lawyer in a law firm with

other lawyers, some of whom are women, he will of course not initiate many of the kinds of discussion that he might with his wife. In fact one of the special initiatives mature masculinity will take is to build protections against the development of any kind of inappropriate intimacy with his female colleagues. It is not *primarily* the responsibility of women to build procedural and relational guidelines to protect themselves from the advances of ill-behaved men. Primarily it is the responsibility of mature manhood to establish a pattern of behaviors and attitudes — a kind of collegial choreography — that enable men and women to move with freedom and ease and moral security among each other.

If, in the course of the day, a woman in the law firm calls a meeting of the attorneys, and thus takes that kind of initiative, there are still ways that a man, coming to that meeting, can express his manhood through culturally appropriate courtesies shown to the women in the firm. He may open the door; he may offer his chair; he may speak in a voice that is gentler.[17]

It is true that this becomes increasingly difficult where a unisex mentality converts such gentlemanly courtesies into offenses and thus attempts to shut out every means of expressing the realities of manhood and womanhood. It will be a strain for mature Christian men and women to work in that atmosphere. But it may be that through intelligent discussion and courteous, caring behaviors they may have a redeeming effect even on what their colleagues think and feel about manhood and womanhood.

We must reckon with the possibility that in the various spheres of life it is possible that role relationships emerge for men and women that so deeply compromise what a man or woman senses is appropriate for their masculine or feminine personhood that they have to seek a different position. This is what J. I. Packer implies when he makes the following perceptive observation:

> While I am not keen on *hierarchy* and *patriarchy* as terms describing the man-woman relationship in Scripture, Genesis 2:18-23 . . . and Ephesians 5:21-33 . . . continue to convince me that the man-woman relationship is intrinsically nonreversible. By this I mean that, other things being equal, a situation in which a female boss has a male secretary, or a marriage in which the woman (as we say) wears the trousers, will put more strain on the humanity of both parties than if it were the other way around. This is part of the reality of the creation, a given fact that nothing will change.[18]

This brings us back to the basic insight of Paul Jewett, namely, that

> Our self-knowledge is indissolubly bound up not simply with our *human* being but with our *sexual* being. At the human level there is no 'I and thou' *per se*, but only the 'I' who is male or female confronting the 'thou,' the 'other,' who is also male or female.

I believe this is true and that God has not left us without a witness to the meaning of our masculine and feminine personhood. I have tried to unfold at least some of what that masculine personhood involves. Now we turn to the meaning of mature femininity.

3

The Meaning of Femininity

A significant aspect of femininity is a way of responding to the pattern of initiatives established by mature masculinity. This is why I have discussed masculinity first. Much of the meaning of womanhood is clearly implied in what I have said already about manhood—in the same way that the moves of one ballet dancer would be implied if you described the moves of the other. Nevertheless it is important now to focus on the description of womanhood given earlier and unfold its meaning for the sake of a balanced and attractive portrait of manhood and womanhood.

AT THE HEART OF MATURE FEMININITY IS A FREE-ING DISPOSITION TO AFFIRM, RECEIVE AND NURTURE STRENGTH AND LEADERSHIP FROM

WORTHY MEN IN WAYS APPROPRIATE TO A
WOMAN'S DIFFERING RELATIONSHIPS.[19]

"AT THE HEART OF . . ."

Again, this phrase signals that the definition of femininity is
not exhaustive. There is more to femininity, but not less. I
believe this is at the heart of what true womanhood means,
even if there is a mystery to our complementary existence that
we will never exhaust.

". . . MATURE FEMININITY . . ."

The word "mature" implies that there are distortions of femininity. False or immature stereotypes are sometimes identified
as the essence of femininity. Ronda Chervin, in her book
Feminine, Free and Faithful, gives a list of what people com-
monly consider "positive feminine traits" and "negative feminine traits." The participants in her workshops say positively
that women are

> responsive, compassionate, empathetic, enduring, gen-
> tle, warm, tender, hospitable, receptive, diplomatic, con-
> siderate, polite, supportive, intuitive, wise, perceptive,
> sensitive, spiritual, sincere, vulnerable (in the sense of
> emotionally open), obedient, trusting, graceful, sweet,
> expressive, charming, delicate, quiet, sensually receptive
> (vs. prudish), faithful, pure.

Chervin lists the following women who exhibit many of these traits: Ruth, Naomi, Sarah, Mary (Jesus' mother), Cordelia of *King Lear,* Melanie in *Gone with the Wind,* Grace Kelly, and Mother Teresa of Calcutta. On the other hand people often stereotype women with negative traits:

> weak, passive, slavish, weepy, wishy-washy, seductive, flirtatious, vain, chatter-box, silly, sentimental, naive, moody, petty, catty, prudish, manipulative, complaining, nagging, pouty, smothering, spiteful.[20]

It is plain then that when we talk of femininity we must make careful distinctions between distortions and God's original design. "Mature femininity" refers not to what sin has made of womanhood or what popular opinion makes of it, but what God willed for it to be at its best.

". . . IS A FREEING DISPOSITION . . ."

I focus on mature femininity as a *disposition* rather than a set of behaviors or roles because mature femininity will express itself in so many different ways depending on the situation. Hundreds of behaviors may be feminine in one situation and not in another. And the specific acts that grow out of the disposition of womanhood vary considerably from relationship to relationship, not to mention from culture to culture.

For example, the Biblical reality of a wife's submission would take different forms depending on the quality of a husband's leadership. This can be seen best if we define submission not in terms of specific behaviors, but as a *disposition* to yield to the husband's authority and an *inclination* to follow his leadership.[21] This is important to do because no submission of one human being to another is absolute. The husband does not replace Christ as the woman's supreme authority. She must never follow her husband's leadership into sin. She will not steal with him or get drunk with him or savor pornography with him or develop deceptive schemes with him.

But even where a Christian wife may have to stand with Christ against the sinful will of her husband, she can still have a spirit of submission—a disposition to yield. She can show by her attitude and behavior that she does not like resisting his will and that she longs for him to forsake sin and lead in righteousness so that her disposition to honor him as head can again produce harmony.[22]

The disposition of mature femininity is experienced as freeing. This is because it accords with the truth of God's purpose in creation. It is the truth that frees (John 8:32). There are sensations of unbounded independence that are not true freedom because they deny truth and are destined for calamity. For example, two women may jump from an airplane and experience the thrilling freedom of free-falling. But there is a difference: one is encumbered by a parachute on her back and the other is free from this burden. Which person is most free? The one without the parachute feels free—even freer, since she does not feel the constraints of the parachute straps. But she is not truly free. She is in bondage to the force of gravity and to the deception that all is well because she feels unencumbered. This false sense of freedom is in fact bondage to calamity which is sure to happen after a fleeting moment of pleasure.

That is the way many women (and men) today think of freedom. They judge it on the basis of immediate sensations of unrestrained license or independence. But true freedom takes God's reality and God's purpose for creation into account and seeks to fit smoothly into God's good design. Freedom does include doing what we want to do. But the mature and wise woman does not seek this freedom by bending reality to fit her desires. She seeks it by being transformed in the renewal of her desires to fit in with God's perfect will (Romans 12:2). The greatest freedom is found in being so changed by God's Spirit that you can do what you love to do and know that it conforms to the design of God and leads to life and glory.

God does not intend for women to be squelched or cramped or frustrated. But neither does he intend for women to do whatever seems to remove these feelings without regard to the appropriateness of the action. Sometimes freedom comes from outward changes in circumstances. Sometimes it comes from inward changes of the heart and mind. Many today say, for example, that true freedom for a lesbian would be the liberty to act according to her sexual preference.[23] But

I would say that true freedom cannot ignore God's judgment on homosexual activity and God's will for men and women to be heterosexual in their sexual relations. Therefore true freedom is not giving in to our every impulse. It is the sometimes painful and exhilarating discovery of God's power to fight free from the bondage of our sinful selves.[24]

I believe that the femininity to which God calls women is the path of freedom for every woman. It will not look the same in every woman. But it will lay responsibilities on all women in the same way that mature masculinity lays responsibilities on all men. Some of these we express very naturally. Others of them we must grow into by prayer and faith and practice. But this process of growth is no more confining than the growth of a young woman toward patterns of mature behavior that enable her to act with natural freedom in the company of adults.

". . . TO AFIRM, RECEIVE AND NURTURE STRENGTH AND LEADERSHIP FROM WORTHY MEN . . ."

"At the heart of mature femininity is a freeing disposition *to affirm, receive and nurture strength and leadership from worthy men* in ways appropriate to a woman's differing relationships."

The "strength and leadership" referred to here is what was described above concerning the responsibility of mature masculinity to lead, provide and protect. The quality of that strength and leadership is captured in the phrase, "from worthy men." I recognize that there is strength and leadership that is unworthy of a woman's affirmation. I do not mean to define femininity merely as a response to whatever sinful men may happen to offer up. Mature femininity is rooted in a commitment to Christ as Lord and is discerning in what it approves. Mature femininity has a clear, Biblical vision of mature masculinity. Woman delights in it as man delights in mature femininity. Each gives the other the greatest scope for natural, pure, mature expression. But when a man does not possess mature masculinity the response of a mature woman is not to abandon her femininity. Rather, her femininity remains intact as a desire for things to be as God intended them to be. But she also recognizes that the natural expression of her womanhood will be hindered by the immaturity of the man in her presence.

My definition of the heart of femininity includes three words to describe the response of a woman to the strength and leadership of worthy men: affirm, receive and nurture.

"Affirm" means that mature women advocate the kind of masculine-feminine complementarity that we are describing here. This is important to stress because there may be occasions when women have no interaction with men and yet are still mature in their femininity. This is because femininity is a disposition to *affirm* the strength and leadership of worthy men, not just to *experience* it firsthand. It is also true, as we will see below, because there are unique feminine strengths and insights that women embody even before they can be given to any man.

"Receive" means that mature femininity feels natural and glad to accept the strength and leadership of worthy men.[25] A mature woman is glad when a respectful, caring, upright man offers sensitive strength and provides a pattern of appropriate initiatives in their relationship. She does not want to reverse these roles. She is glad when he is not passive. She feels herself enhanced and honored and freed by his caring strength and servant-leadership.

"Nurture" means that a mature woman senses a responsibility not merely to receive, but to nurture and strengthen the resources of masculinity. She is to be his partner and assistant. She joins in the act of strength and shares in the process of leadership. She is, as Genesis 2:18 says, "a helper suitable for him."

This may sound paradoxical—that she strengthens the strength she receives, and that she refines and extends the leadership she looks for. But it is not contradictory or unintelligible. There are strengths and insights that women bring to a relationship that are not brought by men. I do not mean to imply by my definition of femininity that women are merely recipients in relation to men. Mature women bring nurturing strengths and insights that make men stronger and wiser and that make the relationship richer.[26]

Note: We need to heed a caution here about the differing strengths of men and women. Whenever anyone asks if we think women are, say, weaker than men, or smarter than men, or more easily frightened than men or something like that, a good answer would go like this: women are weaker in some ways and men are weaker in some ways; women are smarter in some ways and men are smarter in some ways; women are more easily frightened in some kinds of circumstances and men are more easily frightened in other kinds of circumstances.

It is very misleading to put negative values on the so-called weaknesses that each of us has by virtue of our sexuality. God intends for all the "weaknesses" that are characteristically masculine to call forth and highlight woman's strengths. And God intends for all the "weaknesses" that are characteristically feminine to call forth and highlight man's strengths.

A person who naively assumes that men are superior because of their kind of strength might consider these statistics from 1983: six times more men than women are arrested for drug abuse. Ten times more men than women are arrested for drunkenness. 83% of serious crimes in America are committed by men. Twenty-five times more men than women are in jail. Virtually all rape is committed by men.[27]

I point that out to show that boasting in either sex as superior to the other is a folly. Men and women as God created them are different in hundreds of ways. One helpful way to describe our equality and differences is this: Picture the so-called weaknesses and strengths of man and woman listed in two columns. If you could give a numerical value to each one the sum at the bottom of both columns is going to be the same. Whatever different minuses and pluses are on each side of masculinity and femininity are going to balance out. And when you take those two columns from each side and lay them, as it were, on top of each other, God intends them to be the perfect complement to each other, so that when life together is considered (and I don't just mean married life) the weaknesses of manhood are not weaknesses and the weaknesses of woman are not weaknesses. They are the complements that call forth different strengths in each other.[28]

If it is true that manhood and womanhood are to complement rather than duplicate each other, and if it is true that the way God made us is good, then we should be very slow to gather a list of typical male weaknesses or a list of typical female weaknesses and draw a conclusion that either is of less value than the other. Men and women are of equal value and dignity in the eyes of God—both created in the image of God and utterly unique in the universe.[29]

". . . IN WAYS APPROPRIATE TO A WOMAN'S DIFFERING RELATIONSHIPS . . ."

"At the heart of mature femininity is a freeing disposition to affirm, receive and nurture strength and leadership from worthy men *in ways appropriate to a woman's differing relationships.*"

Mature femininity does not express itself in the same way toward every man. A mature woman who is married, for example, does not welcome the same kind of strength and leadership from other men that she welcomes from her husband. But she will affirm and receive and nurture the strength and leadership of men *in some form* in all her relationships with men. This is true even though she may find herself in roles that put some men in a subordinate role to her. Without passing any judgment on the appropriateness of any of these roles one thinks of the following possible instances:

- Prime Minister and her counsellors and advisors.
- Principal and the teachers in her school.
- College teacher and her students.
- Bus driver and her passengers.
- Bookstore manager and her clerks and stock help.
- Staff doctor and her interns.
- Lawyer and her aides.
- Judge and the court personnel.
- Police officer and citizens in her precinct.
- Legislator and her assistants.
- T.V. newscaster and her editors.
- Counsellor and her clients.

One or more of these roles might stretch appropriate expressions of femininity beyond the breaking point. But in any case, regardless of the relationships in which a woman finds herself, mature femininity will seek to express itself in appropriate ways. There are ways for a woman to interact even with a male subordinate that signal to him and others her endorsement of his mature manhood in relationship to her as a woman. I do not have in mind anything like sexual suggestiveness or innuendo. Rather, I have in mind culturally appropriate expressions of respect for his kind of strength, and glad acceptance of his gentlemanly courtesies. Her demeanor—the tone and style and disposition and discourse of her ranking position—can signal clearly her affirmation of the unique role that men should play in relationship to women owing to their sense of responsibility to protect and lead.

It is obvious at this point that we are on the brink of contradiction—suggesting that a woman may hold a position of leadership and fulfill it in a way that signals to men her endorsement of their sense of responsibility to lead. But the complexities of life require of us this risk. To illustrate: it is simply impossible that from time to time a woman not be put in a position of influencing or guiding men. For example, a housewife in her backyard may be asked by a man how to get to the freeway. At that point she is giving a kind of leadership. She has superior knowledge that the man needs and he submits himself to her guidance. But we all know that there is a way for that housewife to direct the man that neither of them feels their mature femininity or masculinity compromised. It is not a contradiction to speak of *certain kinds* of influence coming from women to men in ways that affirm the responsibility of men to provide a pattern of strength and initiative.

But as I said earlier, there are roles that strain the personhood of man and woman too far to be appropriate, productive and healthy for the overall structure of home and society. Some roles would involve kinds of leadership and expectations of authority and forms of strength as to make it unfitting for a woman to fill the role. However, instead of trying to list what jobs might be fitting expressions for mature femininity or mature masculinity, it will probably be wiser to provide several guidelines.

It is obvious that we cannot and should not prohibit women from influencing men. For example, *prayer* is certainly a God-appointed means women should use to get men to where God wants them to be. Praying women exert far more power in this world than all political leaders put together. This kind of powerful influence is compounded immensely when one considers the degree to which the world is shaped and guided by the effects of how men and women are formed by their mothers. This influence is perhaps more effective than all the leadership of men put together.

So the question should be put: what kind of influence would be inappropriate for mature women to exercise toward men? It would be hopeless to try to define this on a case-by-case basis. There are thousands of different jobs in the church and in the world with an innumerable variety of relationships between men and women. More appropriate than a black-and-white list of "man's work" and "woman's work" is a set of criteria to help a woman think through whether the responsibilities of any given job allow her to uphold God's created order of mature masculinity and femininity.

Here is one possible set of criteria. All acts of influence and guidance can be described along these two continuums:

Personal_____Non-personal

Directive_____Non-directive

To the degree that a woman's influence over man is personal and directive it will generally offend a man's good, God-given sense of responsibility and leadership, and thus controvert God's created order.

A woman may design the traffic pattern of a city's streets and thus exert a kind of influence over all male drivers. But this influence will be non-personal and therefore not necessarily an offense against God's order. Similarly, the drawings and specifications of a woman architect may guide the behavior of contractors and laborers, but it may be so non-personal that the feminine-masculine dynamic of the relationship is negligible.

On the other hand, the relationship between husband and wife is very personal. All acts of influence lie on the continuum between personal and impersonal. The closer they get to the personal side, the more inappropriate it becomes for women to exert directive influence.

But the second continuum may qualify the first. Some influence is very directive, some is non-directive. For example, a drill sergeant would epitomize directive influence. It would be hard to see how a woman could be a drill sergeant over men without violating their sense of masculinity and her sense of femininity.

Non-directive influence proceeds with petition and persuasion instead of directives. A beautiful example of non-directive leadership is when Abigail talked David out of killing Nabal (1 Samuel 25:23-35). She exerted great influence over David and changed the course of his life; but she did it with amazing restraint and submissiveness and discretion.

When you combine these two continuums, what emerges is this: If a woman's job involves a good deal of directives toward men, they will, in general, need it to be non-personal.

The God-given sense of responsibility for leadership in a mature man will not generally allow him to flourish long under personal, directive leadership of a female superior. J. I. Packer suggested that "a situation in which a female boss has a male secretary" puts strain on the humanity of both (see note 16). I think this would be true in other situations as well. Some of the more obvious ones would be in military combat settings if women were positioned so as to deploy and command men; or in professional baseball if a woman is made the umpire to call balls and strikes and frequently to settle heated disputes among men. And I would stress that this is not necessarily owing to male egotism, but to a natural and good penchant given by God.

Conversely, if a woman's relation to man is very personal, then the way she offers guidance will need to be non-directive. The clearest example here is the marriage relationship. The Apostle Peter speaks of a good wife's meek and tranquil spirit that can be very winsome to her husband (1 Peter 3:4). A wife who "comes on strong" with her advice will probably drive a husband into passive silence, or into active anger.

It is not nonsense to say that a woman who believes she should guide a man into new behavior should do that in a way that signals her support of his leadership. This is precisely what the Apostle Peter commends in l Peter 3:lff. Similarly in the workplace it may not be nonsense in any given circumstance for a woman to provide a certain kind of direction for a man, but to do it in such a way that she signals her endorsement of his unique duty as a man to feel a responsibility of strength and protection and leadership toward her as a woman and toward women in general.

4

The Biblical Vision of Complementarity

In the book *Recovering Biblical Manhood and Womanhood* (Crossway, 1990) we show, with more detailed exegetical argumentation, that the vision of masculine and feminine complementarity sketched in this essay is a Biblical vision—not a perfect portrayal of it, no doubt, but a faithful one. This is the way God meant it to be before there was any sin in the world: sinless man, full of love, in his tender, strong leadership in relation to woman; and sinless woman, full of love, in her joyful, responsive support for man's leadership. No belittling from the man, no groveling from the woman. Two intelligent, humble, God-entranced beings living out, in beautiful harmony, their unique and different responsibilities. Sin has distorted this purpose at every level. We are not sinless anymore. But we believe that recovery of mature manhood and woman-hood is possible by the power of God's Spirit through faith in his promises and in obedience to his Word.

In the home when a husband leads like Christ and a wife responds like the bride of Christ, there is a harmony and mutuality that is more beautiful and more satisfying than any pattern of marriage created by man. *Biblical headship* for the husband is the divine calling to take primary respon-sibility for Christlike, servant-leadership, protection and provision in the home. *Biblical submission* for the wife is the divine calling to honor and affirm her husband's leadership and help carry it through according to her gifts.[30] This is the way of joy. For God loves his people and he loves his glory. And therefore when we follow his idea of marriage (sketched in texts like Genesis 2:18-24; Proverbs 5:15-19; 31:10-31; Mark 10:2-12; Ephesians 5:21-33; Colossians 3:18-19; and 1 Peter 3:1-7) we are most satisfied and he is most glorified.

The same is true of God's design for the leadership of the church.[31] The realities of headship and submission in mar-riage have their counterparts in the church. Thus Paul speaks of authority and submission in 1 Timothy 2:11-12. We will try to show that *"authority"* refers to the divine call-ing of spiritual, gifted men to take primary responsibility as elders for Christlike servant-leadership and teaching in the church. And *"submission"* refers to the divine calling of the rest of the church, both men and women, to honor and affirm the leadership and teaching of the elders and to be equipped by them for the hundreds and hundreds of various ministries available to men and women in the service of Christ.

That last point is very important. For men and women who have a heart to minister—to save souls and heal broken lives and resist evil and meet needs—there are fields of opportunity that are simply endless. God intends for the entire church to be mobilized in ministry, male and female. Nobody is to be at home watching soaps and ballgames while the world burns. And God intends to equip and mobilize the saints through a company of spiritual men who take primary responsibility for leadership and teaching in the church.

The word "primary" is very important. It signals that there are different kinds and levels of teaching and leading that will not be the sole responsibility of men (Titus 2:3; Proverbs 1:8; 31:26; Acts 18:26). Mature masculinity will seek by prayer and study and humble obedience to discover the pattern of ministry involvement for men and women that taps the gifts of every Christian and honors the God-given order of leadership by spiritual men.

There are many voices today who claim to know a better way to equip and mobilize men and women for the mission of the church. But we believe that manhood and womanhood mesh better in ministry when men take primary responsibility for leadership and teaching in the church; and that mature manhood and womanhood are better preserved, better nurtured, more fulfilled and more fruitful in this church order than in any other.

If I were to put my finger on one devastating sin today, it would not be the so-called women's movement, but the lack of spiritual leadership by men at home and in the church. Satan has achieved an amazing tactical victory by disseminating the notion that the summons for male leadership is born of pride and fallenness, when in fact pride is precisely what prevents spiritual leadership. The spiritual aimlessness and weakness and lethargy and loss of nerve among men is the major issue, not the upsurge of interest in women's ministries.

Pride and self-pity and fear and laziness and confusion are luring many men into self-protecting, self-exalting cocoons of silence. And to the degree that this makes room for women to take more leadership it is sometimes even endorsed as a virtue. But I believe that deep down the men—and the women—know better.

Where are the men with a moral vision for their families, a zeal for the house of the Lord, a magnificent commitment to the advancement of the kingdom, an articulate dream for the mission of the church and a tenderhearted tenacity to make it real?

When the Lord visits us from on high and creates a mighty army of deeply spiritual men committed to the Word of God and global mission, the vast majority of women will rejoice over the leadership of these men and enter into a joyful partnership that upholds and honors the beautiful Biblical pattern of mature manhood and mature womanhood.

5

A Closing Challenge to
Men and Women

Several years ago the women of our church asked for a morning seminar in which I would lay out my vision of manhood and womanhood and discus it with them. I was eager for this opportunity. We spent all of Saturday morning together. It was very encouraging for me. They had many hard questions, but as a whole were wonderfully supportive of the vision I shared. Not all the women of our church see things exactly the same way; but those who came out that Saturday morning were enthusiastic about the kind of manhood and womanhood portrayed in this book.

I closed the seminar with a personal (fifteen-point) challenge to the women of our church. It has some parts that show the special emphases of our fellowship, but I thought it would be a helpful and practical way to conclude this essay. To balance the ledger I have written a corresponding challenge to men. Ten of the points are virtually identical for men and women (1-8, 12-13).

My earnest challenge and prayer for you is . . .

WOMEN	**MEN**
1. That all of your life—in whatever calling—be devoted to the glory of God.	1. That all of your life—in whatever calling—be devoted to the glory of God.
2. That the promises of Christ be trusted so fully that peace and joy and strength fill your soul to overflowing.	2. That the promises of Christ be trusted so fully that peace and joy and strength fill your soul to overflowing.
3. That this fullness of God overflow in daily acts of love so that people might see your good deeds and give glory to your Father in Heaven.	3. That this fullness of God overflow in daily acts of love so that people might see your good deeds and give glory to your Father in Heaven.
4. That you be women of the Book, who love and study and obey the Bible in every area of its teaching. That meditation on Biblical truth	4. That you be men of the Book, who love and study and obey the Bible in every area of its teaching. That meditation on Biblical truth

be the source of hope and faith. That you continue to grow in understanding through all the chapters of your life, never thinking that study and growth are only for others.

5. That you be women of prayer, so that the Word of God will be opened to you, and so the power of faith and holiness will descend upon you, that your spiritual influence may increase at home and at church and in the world.

6. That you be women who have a deep grasp of the sovereign grace of God which undergirds all these spiritual processes; and that you be deep thinkers about the doctrines of grace, and even deeper lovers of these things.

7. That you be totally com-

be the source of hope and faith. That you continue to grow in understanding through all the chapters of your life, never thinking that study and growth are only for others.

5. That you be men of prayer, so that the Word of God will be opened to you, so the power of faith and holiness will descend upon you, that your spiritual influence may increase at home and at church and in the world.

6. That you be men who have a deep grasp of the sovereign grace of God which undergirds all these spiritual processes; and that you be deep thinkers about the doctrines of grace, and even deeper lovers of these things.

7. That you be totally com-

mitted to ministry, whatever your specific calling; that you not fritter your time away on soaps or women's magazines or unimportant hobbies or shopping; that you redeem the time for Christ and his Kingdom.

8. That, if you are single, you exploit your singleness to the full in devotion to God (the way Jesus and Paul and Mary Slessor and Amy Carmichael did) and not be paralyzed by the desire to be married.

9. That, if you are married, you creatively and intelligently and sincerely support the leadership of your husband as deeply as obedience to Christ will allow; that you encourage him in his God-appointed role as head; that you influence him spiritually primarily through your fear-

mitted to ministry, whatever your specific calling; that you not fritter your time away on excessive sports and recreation or unimportant hobbies or aimless diddling in the garage; but that you redeem the time for Christ and his Kingdom.

8. That, if you are single, you exploit your singleness to the full in devotion to God (the way Jesus and Paul and Mary Slessor and Amy Carmichael did) and not be paralyzed by the desire to be married.

9. That, if you are married, you love your wife the way Christ loved the church and gave himself for her; that you be a humble, self-denying, upbuilding, happy spiritual leader; that you consistently grow in grace and knowledge so as never to quench the aspirations of your wife for

less tranquillity and holiness and prayer.

spiritual advancement; that you cultivate tenderness and strength, a pattern of initiative and a listening ear; and that you accept the *responsibility* of provision and protection in the family, however you and your wife share the labor.

10. That, if you have children, you accept responsibility with your husband (or alone if necessary) to raise up children in the discipline and instruction of the Lord—children who hope in the triumph of God—sharing with your husband the teaching and discipline they need, and giving them the special attachment they crave from you, as well as that special nurturing touch and care that you alone are fitted to give.

10. That, if you have children, you accept primary responsibility, in partnership with your wife (or as a single parent), to raise up children in the discipline and instruction of the Lord—children who hope in the triumph of God; that you establish a pattern of teaching and discipline that is not solely dependent on the church or school to impart Bible knowledge and spiritual values to the children; and that you give your children the time and attention and affection

that communicates the true nature of our Father in Heaven.

11. That you not assume that secular employment is a greater challenge or a better use of your life than the countless opportunities of service and witness in the home, the neighborhood, the community, the church, and the world; that you not only pose the question: career or full-time homemaker?, but that you ask just as seriously: full-time career or freedom for ministry? That you ask: Which would be greater for the Kingdom—to work for someone who tells you what to do to make his or her business prosper, or to be God's free agent dreaming your own dream about how your time and your home and your creativity could make God's

11. That you not assume advancement and peer approval in your gainful employment are the highest values in life; but that you ponder the eternal significance of faithful fatherhood and time spent with your wife; that you repeatedly consider the new possibilities at each stage of your life for maximizing your energies for the glory of God in ministry; that you pose the question often: Is our family molded by the culture, or do we embody the values of the Kingdom of God? That you lead the family in making choices not on the basis of secular trends or upward lifestyle expectations, but on the basis of what will

business prosper? And that in all this you make your choices not on the basis of secular trends or upward lifestyle expectations, but on the basis of what will strengthen the faith of the family and advance the cause of Christ.

strengthen the faith of the family and advance the cause of Christ.

12. That you step back and (with your husband, if you are married) plan the various forms of your life's ministry in chapters. Chapters are divided by various things— age, strength, singleness, marriage, employment, children at home, children in college, grandchildren, retirement, etc. No chapter has all the joys. Finite life is a series of trade-offs. Finding God's will, and living for the glory of Christ to the full in every chapter is what makes it a success, not whether it reads

12. That you step back and (with your wife, if you are married) plan the various forms of your life's ministry in chapters. Chapters are divided by various things— age, strength, singleness, marriage, employment, children at home, children in college, grandchildren, retirement, etc. No chapter has all the joys. Finite life is a series of trade-offs. Finding God's will and living for the glory of Christ to the full in every chapter is what makes it a success, not whether it reads

like somebody else's chapter or whether it has in it what only another chapter will bring.

13. That you develop a wartime mentality and lifestyle; that you never forget that life is short, that billions of people hang in the balance of Heaven and Hell every day, that the love of money is spiritual suicide, that the goals of upward mobility (nicer clothes, cars, houses, vacations, food, hobbies) are a poor and dangerous substitute for the goals of living for Christ with all your might and maximizing your joy in ministry to people's needs.

14. That in all your relationships with men (not just in marriage) you seek the guidance of the Holy Spirit in applying the Biblical vision of manhood and womanhood;

like somebody else's chapter or whether it has in it what only another chapter will bring.

13. That you develop a wartime mentality and lifestyle; that you never forget that life is short, that billions of people hang in the balance of Heaven and Hell every day, that the love of money is spiritual suicide, that the goals of upward mobility (nicer clothes, cars, houses, vacations, food, hobbies) are a poor and dangerous substitute for the goals of living for Christ with all your might and maximizing your joy in ministry to people's needs.

14. That in all your relationships with women (not just in marriage) you seek the guidance of the Holy Spirit in applying the Biblical vision of manhood and womanhood;

that you develop a style and demeanor that does justice to the unique role God has given to man to feel responsible for gracious leadership in relation to women—a leadership which involves elements of protection and provision and a pattern of initiative. That you think creatively and with cultural sensitivity (just as he must do) in shaping the style and setting the tone of your interaction with men.

that you develop a style and demeanor that expresses your God-given responsibility for humble strength and leadership, and for self-sacrificing provision and protection; that you think creatively and with cultural sensitivity (just as she must do) in shaping the style and setting the tone of your interaction with women.

15. That you see the Biblical guidelines for what is appropriate and inappropriate for men and women not as arbitrary constraints on freedom, but as wise and gracious prescriptions for how to discover the true freedom of God's ideal of complementarity. That you not measure your potential by the few roles withheld, but by the count-

15. That you see the Biblical guidelines for what is appropriate and inappropriate for men and women not as license for domination or bossy passivity, but as a call to servant-leadership that thinks in terms of responsibilities not rights; that you see these principles as wise and gracious prescriptions for how to discover the true freedom of

less roles offered. That you look to the loving God of Scripture and dream about the possibilities of your service to him, with the following list as possibilities for starters: God's ideal of complementarity; that you encourage the fruitful engagement of women in the countless ministry roles that are Biblically appropriate and deeply needed. For example:

OPPORTUNITIES FOR MINISTRY

Ministries to the handicapped
  Hearing impaired
  Blind
  Lame
  Retarded

Ministries to the sick
  Nursing
  Physician
  Hospice care—cancer, AIDS, etc.
  Community health

Ministries to the socially estranged
  Emotionally impaired
  Recovering alcoholics
  Recovering drug-users
  Escaping prostitutes
  Abused children, women
  Runaways, problem children
  Orphans

Prison ministries
  Women's prisons
  Families of prisoners
  Rehabilitation to society

Audiovisual ministries
  Composition
  Design
  Production
  Distribution

Writing ministries
  Free-lance
  Curriculum development
  Fiction
  Non-fiction
  Editing
  Institutional communications
  Journalistic skills for publications

Teaching ministries
  Sunday school: children, youth,
    students, women
  Grade school
  High school
  College

Music ministries
  Composition
  Training

Ministries to youth
  Teaching
  Sponsoring
  Open houses and recreation
  Outings and trips
  Counseling
  Academic assistance

Sports ministries
  Neighborhood teams
  Church teams

Therapeutic counseling
  Independent
  Church-based
  Institutional

Radio and television ministries
  Technical assistance
  Writing
  Announcing
  Producing

Theater and drama ministries
  Acting
  Directing
  Writing
  Scheduling

Social ministries
  Literacy
  Pro-life
  Pro-decency
  Housing
  Safety
  Beautification
  Drug rehabilitation

Performance
  Voice
  Choir
  Instrumentalist

Evangelistic ministries
  Personal witnessing
  Parachurch groups
  Home Bible studies
  Outreach to children
  Visitation teams
  Counseling at meetings
  Telephone counseling

Pastoral care assistance
  Visitation
  Newcomer welcoming and assistance
  Hospitality
  Food and clothing and transportation

Prayer ministries
  Praying
  Mobilizing for prayer events
  Helping with small groups of prayer
  Coordinating prayer chains
  Promoting prayer days and weeks
    and vigils

Missions
  All of the above across cultures

Support ministries
  Countless "secular" jobs that
    undergird other ministries

The awesome significance of
  motherhood

Making a home as a full-time wife

I realize this list is incomplete and reflects my own culture and limitations. But it is worth the risk, I think, to make clear that the vision of manhood and womanhood presented in this book is not meant to hinder ministry but to purify and empower it in a pattern of Biblical obedience.

The ninth affirmation of the Danvers Statement[32] is perhaps the crucial final thing to say so that the aim of this book is not misunderstood.

> With half the world's population outside the reach of indigenous evangelism; with countless other lost people in those societies that have heard the gospel; with the stresses and miseries of sickness, malnutrition, homelessness, illiteracy, ignorance, aging, addiction, crime, incarceration, neuroses, and loneliness, no man or woman who feels a passion from God to make His grace known in word and deed need ever live without a fulfilling ministry for the glory of Christ and the good of this fallen world.

Notes

1. Between November, 1983 and May, 1984 I carried on a debate concerning this issue with my friends and former colleagues Alvera and Berkeley Mickelsen in our denominational periodical, *The Standard* (of the Baptist General Conference). In these monthly articles I tried to lay the exegetical foundations for how men and women are called by God to relate to each other. The names of the articles are: "Male, Female and Morality" (November, 1983), pp. 26-28; "Satan's Design in Reversing Male Leadership Role" (December, 1983), pp. 33-35; "Jesus' Teaching on Men and Women: Dismantling the Fall, Not the Creation" (January, 1984), pp. 32-34; "A Metaphor of Christ and the Church" (February, 1984), pp. 27-29; "Creation, Culture and Corinthian Prophetesses" (March, 1984), pp. 30-32; "The Order of Creation" (April, 1984), pp. 35-38; "How Should a Woman Lead?" (May, 1984), pp. 34-36.

2. The cassette tapes of seven sermons on manhood and womanhood can be ordered by writing to Council of Biblical Manhood and Womanhood, P.O. Box 1173, Wheaton, IL 60189.

3. Paul K. Jewett, *Man as Male and Female* (Grand Rapids: William B. Eerdmans Pub. Co., 1975), p. 172.

4. *Man as Male and Female*, p. 173. The reference is to Emil Brunner, *Das Gebot und die Ordnungen* (Tuebingen: J.C.B. Mohr, 1933), p. 358.

5. *Man as Male and Female*, p. 178.

6. *Man as Male and Female*, p. 187f.

7. The teaching in 1 Peter 3:1-7 concerning the differentiation of roles is not based explicitly on the order of creation, but neither is it based on convention. Rather it is rooted in the example of "holy women who hoped in God" (v. 5). Sarah is cited as an example of submission, not because she complied with Abraham's wish that she pose as his sister (Genesis 20), which is the amazing example of submission we might have expected Peter to use, but rather because she said "my lord" when speaking offhandedly to herself about her husband. This seems to suggest that the root of Sarah's submission was a deep allegiance to Abraham's leadership that expressed itself without coercion or public pressure.

8. This is developed and defended exegetically in two extensive essays by John Sailhammer and Ray Ortlund Jr. in *Recovering Biblical Manhood and Womanhood* (Crossway Books, 1990).

9. The limitation of this essay is seen, for example, in that I will say very little about the capacity of a woman to bear children, and the special role that she has in nursing and nurturing them. Nor do I say anything about the man's crucial role in nurturing healthy, secure children. My focus is on the significance that manhood and womanhood have for the relational dynamics between men and women and the implications of these dynamics for the roles appropriate for each.

10. The fact that a Christian wife and church member, according to Acts 2:17, may "prophesy" implies, at least, that she may often have ideas and insights that a wise and humble husband and pastor will listen to and adopt. On women and prophecy see Wayne Grudem, *The Gift of Prophecy: In the New Testament and Today* (Wheston: Crossway Books, 1988), pp. 215-225.

11. This understanding of masculine responsibility will be developed, for example, from the way God comes to Adam first after the fall, implying his special responsibility in the failure even though Eve had sinned first. This accords with other pointers in the early chapters of Genesis before the fall that God meant for Adam to have a special responsibility for leadership (establishing a pattern of initiative) in relation to Eve. The sharing of initiatives within that general pattern is implied in the image of Christ and the church as the model for mar-

riage (Ephesians 5:21-33). Christ means for his bride to look to him for leadership, but not to the exclusion of her own thoughtful choices and initiatives in communication and in shared mission.

12. James Dobson, *Straight Talk to Men and Their Wives* (Waco: Word Books, 1980), pp. 64f.

13. Notice the move from "Children, obey your *parents*" in Ephesians 6:1 to "*Fathers* . . . bring them up in the nurture and discipline of the Lord" (v. 4). Both have responsibility to discipline, and children should hold both in high regard. But there is a special responsibility on fathers for the moral life and discipline of the home.

14. The Biblical teaching on nature's voice urging men and women not to exchange or confuse the cultural symbols of masculinity and femininity is very relevant here. When Paul says in 1 Corinthians 11:14, "Does not *nature teach* you that for a man to wear long hair is degrading to him?" he means that there is in man a *native sense* of repugnance against taking on cultural symbols of femininity. We would say, "Does not nature teach you that it is degrading to a man to wear a dress to church?" This voice of "nature" has great social benefits even in cultures untouched by special revelation from Scripture. But Romans 1:18-32 shows that a culture can become so corrupted that the native sense is ignored (vv. 26-27) and suppressed so that unnatural practices are even approved (v. 32). At such a point the call for Biblical repentance is not only a call to believe what the Bible teaches, but also to be transformed so deeply that the natural inclinations of mature manhood and womanhood are recovered, and society conforms once again not merely to what the Scriptures teach, but to "what nature teaches" among those who are now under the sway of Biblical truth and, more widely, under the rectifying social power of common grace. Alongside this teaching on the voice of nature should be put the teaching of 1 Corinthians 13:5 that love does not act in an "unseemly" way; it does not offend against good manners.

15. Another pointer from Scripture that this is the way God intends the relationship of husband and wife to be is the image of Christ as head of the church with man playing that role toward his wife according to Ephesians 5:23. The image of head implies that Christ is the *provider* as well as a leader. "Hold fast to the *Head, from whom the whole body,*

nourished and knit together through its joints and ligaments, grows with a growth that is from God" (Colossians 2:19; cf. Ephesians 4:16). This does not at all contradict the idea of leadership implied in "headship." On the contrary it strengthens it. The thought in Colossians 2:19 begins in verse 18 with a reference to people who are puffed up, "not holding fast to the Head, from whom the whole body, nourished and knit together through its joints and ligaments, grows with a growth that is from God." What is especially significant here for us is the implication that since Christ as head is *supplier*, the church must "hold fast" to him. The opposite of holding fast is being puffed up in mind and independent of Christ. So the implication is that headship is a role to be depended on and followed. There is to be an allegiance to the head as provider. This in essence implies a kind of leadership role for the head, as one to whom the body should ever look for what it needs. This is all the more evident when we note how Christ in fact does provide for his wife, the church. As the head he provides the body with truth (Ephesians 4:15, 21) and strength (Colossians 1:11) and wisdom (Colossians 2:3) and love (Ephesians 3:17-18; 4:16; Colossians 2:2). This means that the idea of provider implies loving leader because Christ leads with his truth and wisdom and he does this with love that lives out his teaching before us and for us.

There are numerous other Biblical evidences of the father's special responsibility to provide for his family. Consider, for example, 1 Timothy 3:5, "For if someone (an elder) does not know how to manage *(proistenai)* his own household, how shall he take care of *(epimelesetai)* the church of God?" This idea of managing his own home well may have more than provision in mind (leadership for sure; see the use of *proistemi* in 1 Thessalonians 5:12), but I doubt that it has less. Elders/overseers are responsible to feed (1 Peter 5:2; Acts 20:28; Jeremiah 3:15) and protect (Acts 20:28-31) the flock.

Other evidences of the father's special responsibility to provide for his family portray the husband and father as the protector too. For example, Deuteronomy 10:18, "[God] executes justice for the fatherless and the widow, and loves the stranger giving him food and raiment." In other words, when the natural protector and provider is not there God steps in to take his place for the orphan and widow. Jeremiah 31:32 points in this same direction. God says concerning Israel, "My covenant which they broke, though I was their husband, says the Lord." How was he their husband? The context suggests that he was their husband in giving them protection at the sea and the provision in the wilderness.

16. The Biblical support for this is seen first in the texts like the ones cited above in note 10 (Deuteronomy 10:18 and Jeremiah 31:32). It is also implied in Ephesians 5:25, "Husbands, love your wives as Christ loved the church and gave himself up for her." Christ is here sacrificing himself to protect his wife, the church, from the ravages of sin and hell. Christ gives himself as the model for the husband in this regard because the husband is the *man*. This is not an arbitrary assignment. It is fitting because men were *created* for this. The "mystery" of marriage (Ephesians 5:32) is the truth that God designed male and female from the beginning to carry different responsibilities on the analogy of Christ and his church. The sense of responsibility to protect is there in man by virtue of this design of creation, not by virtue of the marriage covenant. Marriage makes the burden more personal and more intense, but it does not create it.

    Additional support for man's primary responsibility to protect women is found in the Old Testament pattern of men, rather than women, being given the duty to go to war. And nature itself seems to teach this duty of protection by endowing men, by and large, with greater brute strength.

17. Such customs, like all manners, are easily caricatured and satirized. But that is a mark of immaturity. Just as men and women know that some rough contact sports are not natural for women to play, so we know that there is a verbal rough-and-tumble among men, a kind of tough and rugged argumentation that is less appropriate when speaking to a woman than to a man.

18. J. I. Packer, "Understanding the Differences," in *Women, Authority and the Bible,* ed. by Alvera Mickelsen (Downers Grove: InterVarsity Press, 1986), p. 298-299.

19. One way of relating this definition to Scripture is to see it as an attempt to unfold some of what is implied in the old-fashioned phrase

"help meet" in Genesis 2:18—"And the Lord God said, It is not good that the man should be alone; I will make him a help meet for him" (KJV). It may well be that the feminine inclination to help a man in his life and work signifies far more than I have been able to spell out in the phrases "affirm, receive, and nurture." But I have chosen to focus on what seems to me to be the heart of woman's feminine suitableness to man as a helper. The animals were helpful in some ways (Genesis 2:19). But the helpfulness of the woman is radically different. That unique human element is what I am interested in.

20. Ronda Chervin, *Feminine, Free and Faithful* (San Francisco: Ignatius Press, 1986), p. 15.

21. The Biblical warrant for this definition is 1 Peter 3:1-6, where a believing wife is married to an unbelieving husband. The text clearly teaches that she is to be submissive, but not in such a way that follows him in his unbelief. In fact, she is instructed how to get him to change, and be converted. The implication here is that her submission is not a de facto yielding to all that he says (since she has a higher allegiance to Jesus), but a *disposition* to yield and an *inclination* to follow. Her submission is a readiness to support his leadership wherever it does not lead to sin.

22. This paragraph is taken largely from my wider discussion of this issue in *Desiring God* (Portland: Multnomah Press, 1986), pp. 177-184.

23. For example, Gerald Sheppard, a professor of Old Testament at the University of Toronto, said in 1986, "I believe that the Gospel—as Evangelicals Concerned recognizes—should lead us at least to an affirmation of gay and lesbian partnerships ruled by a biblical ethic analogous to that offered for heterosexual relationships." "A Response to Anderson (II)," *TSF Bulletin*, Vol. 9, No. 4, (March-April, 1986), p. 21. Similarly in July of 1986 the Evangelical Women's Caucus International under the influence of Virginia Mollenkott and Nancy Hardesty took a stand affirming the legitimacy of lesbianism to such an extent that members like Katherine Kroeger and Gretchen Hull withdrew their membership. See "Gay Rights Resolution Divides Membership of Evangelical Women's Caucus," in: *Christianity Today* (October 3, 1986), pp. 40-44. Ralph Blair, the founder of Evangelicals Concerned, continues to debunk the claim that homosexuals can or

should change their sexual orientation. He promotes monogamous homosexual relationships and claims Biblical support for it, arguing that the Bible is opposed to promiscuous homosexuality, not homosexuality itself. His views are cited by Tim Stafford, "Coming Out," *Christianity Today* (August 18, 1989), p. 19.

24. For a discussion of contemporary ministries that believe in the real possibilities of homosexuals to experience significant changes in the focus and power of their sexual preference see *Christianity Today*, August 18, 1989. See also George Rekers, *Shaping Your Child's Sexual Identity* (Grand Rapids: Baker Book House, 1982).

25. This is implied in the goodness and gladness of creation before the fall (Genesis 2) when man, created first, was called to the primary responsibility of leadership, and woman, created to be "a helper suitable for him," was called to use her gifts in helping carry that leadership through. This was all "very good" (Genesis 1:31) and therefore must have given man and woman great gladness. The same glad responsiveness to this order of things is implied in Ephesians 5:21-33 where man and wife are to model their relationship after that of Christ and the church. The church delights to accept strength and leadership from Christ. The delight that a woman takes in the strength and leadership of her husband is not merely owing to the marriage covenant. Just as man was created with a native sense of responsibility to lead and provide and protect in ways appropriate to his varying relationships (see note 12), so woman was created as a suitable complement to honor this responsibility with gladness and satisfaction.

26. See page 50 for some examples of feminine strengths that enrich men.

27. Weldon M. Hardenbrook, *Missing from Action: Vanishing Manhood in America* (Nashville: Thomas Nelson Publishers, 1987), pp. 9-10.

28. Experience and psychology teach us that there are significant differences of many kinds between men and women. In each case one could establish a standard that would make one sex stronger and the other weaker. But Paul's teaching on the body of Christ warns us against demeaning those that have traits of weakness—male or female (1 Corinthians 12:21-26). The creation of male and female in the image of God (Genesis 1:27) forbids that we make our diversity a ground for variable worth as persons in God's eyes. And the Biblical

declaration that all was "very good" when God created us with our differences means that a "weakness" by one narrow standard is a
"strength" in its contribution to the total fabric of man as male and
female in God's image.

29. When 1 Peter 3:7 refers to the wife as a "weaker feminine vessel," it
    is probably focussing on the most obvious fact, especially in that more
    rugged culture, that a woman has lesser brute strength. That is, she is
    more in need of protection and provision from the man than he is
    from her. He is to "recognize" this and honor her by supplying all she
    needs as a fellow-heir of grace. The verse does not contemplate the
    question I have raised, namely whether there are some other things
    about man that can also be described as weaker than woman.

30. I am assuming implicitly here what I said about submission on
    pp. 51-52.

31. The elders are charged with the primary responsibility of leadership
    (Acts 20:28; 1 Timothy 5:17; 1 Peter 5:3) and Biblical instruction
    (Titus 1:9; 1 Timothy 3:2; 5:17) in the church. That's a summary of
    their job. So when Paul puts those two things together and says, "I do
    not permit a woman to teach or exercise authority," one very natural
    implication is, "I do not permit a woman to assume the office of elder
    in the church."

    So the authority Paul has in mind in 1 Timothy 2:12 at least
    includes the authority of elders. We saw already from Jesus in Luke
    22:26 what that is supposed to look like: "Let the greatest among you
    become as the youngest, and the leader as one who serves." Paul said
    in 2 Corinthians 10:8 and 13:10 that God gave him authority in the
    church not for tearing down or destroying, but for building up. And
    Peter said to the elders of the churches (1 Peter 5:3), "Do not domi-
    neer over the those in your charge, but be examples to the flock."

    In other words elder-authority is servant-authority. Elder-lead-
    ership is servant-leadership. That's why teaching is at the heart of this
    calling. Biblical authority leads by persuasion—by teaching—not by
    coercion or political maneuvering. Elder-authority is always subordi-
    nate to Biblical truth. Therefore teaching is the primary instrument of
    leadership in the church. And authority refers to the divine calling of
    spiritual, gifted men to take primary responsibility as elders for

Christlike, servant-leadership and teaching in the church. Their goal is not their own status or honor. Their goal is the equipping of the saints—women and men—to do the work of the ministry.

32. The Danvers Statement is the charter statement (Rationale, Purposes and Affirmations) of the Council on Biblical Manhood and Womanhood and may be ordered from the Council at P.O. Box 1173, Wheaton, IL 60189.

A NOTE ON RESOURCES

DESIRING GOD MINISTRIES

If you would like to ponder further the vision of God and life presented in this book, we at Desiring God Ministries (DGM) would love to help you. DGM is a resource ministry of Bethlehem Baptist Church in Minneapolis, Minnesota. Our desire is to fan the flame of your passion for God and help you spread that passion to others. We have hundreds of resources available for this purpose. Most of our inventory consists of books and audiotapes by John Piper. We also maintain a large collection of free articles, sermon manuscripts, and audio messages at our web site. In addition, we produce God-centered children's curricula, host conferences, and coordinate John Piper's conference speaking schedule.

Since money is not our treasure we try to keep our prices as low as possible. And since we don't want money to be a hindrance to the Gospel, if our prices are more than you can pay at this time, our *whatever-you-can-afford* policy applies to almost all of our resources—even if you can't afford to pay anything! We also accept VISA, MasterCard, Discover, and American Express credit cards for convenience and speed, but we would rather give you resources than have you go into debt.

DGM exists to help you make God your treasure. Because God is most glorified in you when you are most satisfied in him.

For more information, call to request a free resource catalog or browse our online store at *www.desiringGOD.org.*

DESIRING GOD MINISTRIES
720 Thirteenth Avenue South
Minneapolis, Minnesota 55415-1793

Toll free in the USA: 1-888-346-4700
International calls: (612) 373-0651
Bethlehem Baptist Church: (612) 338-7653
Fax: (612) 338-4372
mail@desiring GOD.org
www.desiringGOD.org

DESIRING GOD MINISTRIES
UNITED KINGDOM
23 Ashburn Avenue
Waterside, Londonderry
Northern Ireland BT46 5QE

Tel/fax: (02871) 342 907
desiringGOD@UK-Europe.freeserve.co.uk

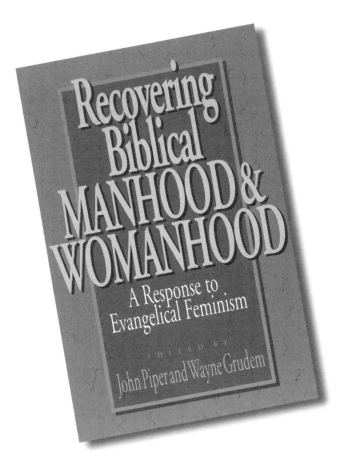

Feminist ideology is everywhere. It's in schools, television shows, music, politics—even the church. In fact, it's so pervasive within the evangelical community that it's become its own movement— "evangelical feminism." But what many of its adherents fail to recognize is that incorporating feminism into theology has devastating implications on our relationships, society, the church, and our homes.

In the most comprehensive response yet, a group of scholars explore every key passage of Scripture to determine the biblical view of male and female roles and relationships. What they have found is imperative for anyone searching for the truth.